AVAILABLE NOW
from Lerner Publishing Services!

The *On the Hardwood* series:

Chicago Bulls
Dallas Mavericks
Los Angeles Clippers
Los Angeles Lakers
Miami HEAT
Minnesota Timberwolves
Oklahoma City Thunder
San Antonio Spurs

COMING SOON!

Additional titles in
the *On the Hardwood* series:

Boston Celtics
Brooklyn Nets
Houston Rockets
Indiana Pacers
New York Knicks
Philadelphia 76ers
Portland Trail Blazers
Utah Jazz

ON THE HARDWOOD

MIAMI HEAT

JOSH ANDERSON

On the Hardwood: Miami HEAT

MVP Books
2255 Calle Clara
La Jolla, CA 92037

MVP Books is an imprint of Book Buddy Digital Media, Inc., 42982 Osgood Road, Fremont, CA 94539

MVP Books publications may be purchased for
educational, business, or sales promotional use.

Cover and layout design by Jana Ramsay
Copyedited by Susan Sylvia
Photos by Getty Images

ISBN: 978-1-61570-501-6 (Library Binding)
ISBN: 978-1-61570-500-9 (Soft Cover)

TABLE OF CONTENTS

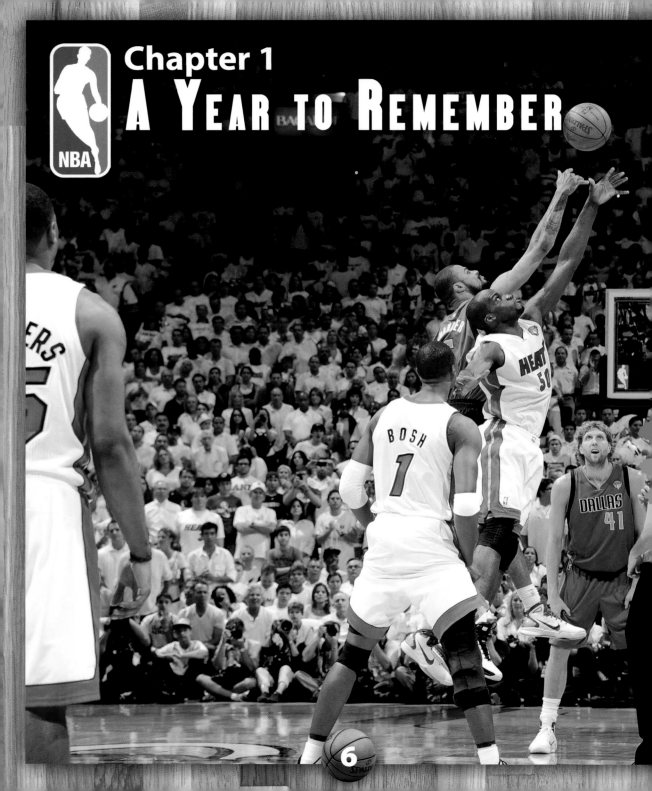

Chapter 1

A Year to Remember

It was Game 6 of the 2011 NBA Finals. The Dallas Mavericks held a 3-2 lead over the Miami HEAT. If the HEAT could find a way to win this game, the series would be tied. They would have a chance to win the NBA Championship a few nights later.

But, if the HEAT lost, the Mavs would celebrate their title in front of the loyal fans in Miami. None of the HEAT players wanted to lose in the Finals, especially on their home court.

Any kid who's ever played basketball dreams about playing in a game like this. Twenty thousand fans roared above the HEAT's home court at AmericanAirlines Arena in Miami, Florida. Nearly every spectator wore a white shirt, a tradition that started in Miami during the 2004 NBA Playoffs. Fans practically begged the HEAT to find a way to win the game. Celebrities like Usher and NBA legend Bill Russell sat courtside.

The HEAT were behind for most of the game, but they arrived at a turning point with about 10 minutes left.

Fans dressed for a "white-out" cheer for the HEAT.

After a run late in the third quarter, the Mavericks came into the fourth quarter leading by nine. But the HEAT started the fourth quarter strong.

Miami had just pulled within four points after young point guard Mario Chalmers swished two big free throws. The score was 81-77. The HEAT desperately needed a "stop" on defense.

Mavericks' point guard, J.J. Barea, dribbled the ball up the court. Barea used a pick and a stutter-step to shake off his defender, HEAT guard Eddie House.

Barea found himself with room, and jumped, releasing his shot. The ball seemed to hang in the air forever. Everyone in the building held their breath...

For fans of the HEAT, this was just the kind of moment to make you think, "How did we get here?" Playing in the NBA Finals was a crazy ending to a crazy year for the Miami HEAT franchise.

Chalmers eyes the basket in preparation for a free throw against the Mavericks.

One year earlier, Coach Erik Spoelstra and team president, Pat Riley, thought a lot about which players to sign during free agency to improve the team.

Coming off of two straight first-round losses in the playoffs, they knew they needed to re-sign their best player, Dwyane Wade. After that, the HEAT set their sights on Chris Bosh and LeBron James.

Bosh was an All-Star forward who had played for the Toronto Raptors. His shooting skill was unusual for a player who stood almost seven feet tall. Signing him would give the

No one can question Dwyane Wade's heart.

HEAT a strong presence in the "low post," the area closest to the basket.

On the same day Wade announced he would stay with the HEAT, Chris Bosh announced he would come to Miami as well.

Roster Turnover
The only HEAT players left from the 2005-06 Championship team in 2010-11 were Dwyane Wade and Udonis Haslem.

9

"King" Without a Crown

LeBron James had an unsuccessful second trip to the NBA Finals in 2011. The Miami HEAT lost in six games.

LeBron James spent his first seven seasons with the Cleveland Cavaliers. Many people considered him to be the greatest player in the NBA. Although he had accomplished a lot on the court, he hadn't won an NBA Championship. As a free agent, James wanted to go to the team that would give him the best chance to win.

One day after Bosh announced he was coming to Miami, LeBron James went on television to announce "The Decision."

James famously told the world: "I'm going to take my talents to South Beach and join the Miami HEAT." The sports media and fans named Wade, Bosh and James, Miami's "Big Three." In the instant LeBron announced he was going to the HEAT, the eyes of the country became focused on Miami.

The day after "The Decision," fans and players celebrated the

LeBron James rises and fires over the Celtics' Marquis Daniels.

new additions to their team at AmericanAirlines Arena.

Based on the talent on their roster, the HEAT looked like one of the best teams in the NBA. HEAT fans hoped that this would be a championship season in Miami. But, things didn't start out exactly as planned...

After the season's first month, the HEAT had a record of 9-8. These results were average, but more was expected of a team with so much talent.

Just as everyone wondered, "What's wrong with the HEAT?" everything changed. The HEAT won 21 out of their next 22 games. They finished with 58 wins, good for first place in the Southeast Division.

The HEAT advanced through the first three rounds of the playoffs. They defeated the Philadelphia 76ers and the Boston Celtics. Then, they beat the Chicago Bulls in the Eastern Conference Finals.

Chris Bosh maneuvers the ball around Chicago's Carlos Boozer in the 2011 NBA Playoffs.

The Mavericks' point guard J.J. Barea shoots over the HEAT's Eddie House.

After five games, the HEAT found themselves down three games to two. The HEAT faced a "must-win" situation in Game 6 of the Finals.

Back to the game's turning point, with about 10 minutes left in the fourth quarter:

As many HEAT fans remember, Mavs' guard J.J. Barea dribbled up the court, used a pick and a stutter-step, and elevated from behind the three-point line. His three-pointer gave Dallas a seven-point lead. It was a crushing blow to the HEAT.

Although Miami would have plenty of other chances during the fourth quarter, the HEAT would never get as close as four points again.

Miami lost the game, 105-95, and

The HEAT would now face a familiar opponent in the 2011 NBA Finals, the Dallas Mavericks. The HEAT had played the Mavericks five years earlier in the Finals. It had been a thrilling six-game series. Would this series live up to that one?

the Mavericks celebrated in Miami.

For Miami, an elimination on their home floor provided all the motivation they needed during the off-season. The HEAT hoped that at the end of the 2011-12 season, they would be the ones celebrating an NBA Championship.

Although the HEAT had a good season, no one was satisfied.

HEAT Coach Erik Spoelstra talked after the game about the mood of his players. "There's certainly an emptiness right now with our group. We've been through a heck of a lot this season, where in many ways it felt like two seasons built in one," he said.

"There's no excuses. There's no blame. Sometimes you simply come up short. All of the storylines and noise out there, that had nothing to do with this series and the outcome," Spoelstra said. "But it doesn't make it feel any easier for the guys in the locker room."

Coach Erik Spoelstra addresses the media after losing to the Mavericks.

Chapter 2
A HUMBLE BEGINNING

The HEAT have been one of the most successful NBA teams in recent years. But, it wasn't always that way. In fact, there was no NBA team in Miami at all until 1987.

That year, the NBA decided to add three teams to the league. An expansion committee was formed to choose the cities that would get teams. Charlotte, North Carolina, and Minneapolis, Minnesota, were chosen. The last spot would go to either Orlando, or Miami, Florida. But, the committee couldn't decide.

For a few days, the people of each city waited anxiously for a decision. Then, a decision came. The NBA would add four teams, instead of three. There would be teams in Orlando *and* Miami.

There was a contest among fans

to come up with a name for the new Miami team. The team owners would pick the best as the winner.

The names the owners liked best were: The Miami Flamingos, The Miami Waves, The Miami Palms, The Miami Sharks, The Miami Manatees, and The Miami HEAT.

Of course, the owners chose "HEAT" as the name, and the team was almost ready to play. But, they still needed players to wear their new red, white, and black uniforms.

In June of 1988, the HEAT participated in an expansion draft where new teams choose players to take away from other teams. Existing teams were allowed to protect eight players each. Protecting a player meant that the new teams could not select him.

The HEAT selected 12 players in the expansion draft. But, only four of the players they chose ever played for the team.

The HEAT had six selections in the 1988 NBA Draft. In preparing for the NBA Draft, all teams search the country for players who will make their squad better.

Miami chose 6'11" center Rony Seikaly with their first pick. Seikaly was born in the country of Lebanon in the Middle East. Seikaly moved to the United States for college and was a star for the Syracuse Orangemen.

Seikaly played for the HEAT for six years, before moving on to other teams. Although he wasn't quite a star player, he was a solid contributor to the team.

Most NBA teams have, at most, two or three rookies on their roster. During their first season, ten different rookies played for the HEAT. The HEAT even had a rookie coach named Ron Rothstein.

The HEAT's original owner Lew Shaffel talks with reporters.

Fans in Miami were very excited about having a team, but they were not very good in their first year. The HEAT set an NBA record by losing their first 17 games.

In the 18th game in franchise history, players and coaches hoped their game against the Clippers would end differently. The HEAT played well early and held a 12-point lead in the third quarter. It looked like it might finally be the night.

But, over the course of the fourth quarter, the Clippers cut into the HEAT's lead. Miami guard Rory Sparrow, one of the best players on those early HEAT teams, remembers the moment like this:

"(We) worried that this game was slipping away like so many others,"

The HEAT's Rory Sparrow was determined to help the team get their first win.

he said. "I wanted to make sure that didn't happen, so when I got open at the foul line, I stuck a jumper to give us the lead, 89-86."

The Clippers quickly answered Sparrow's basket and cut the lead to one point, 89-88. The HEAT tried to

Big Man from Lebanon
Rony Seikaly is one of only two NBA players born in the Middle Eastern country of Lebanon.

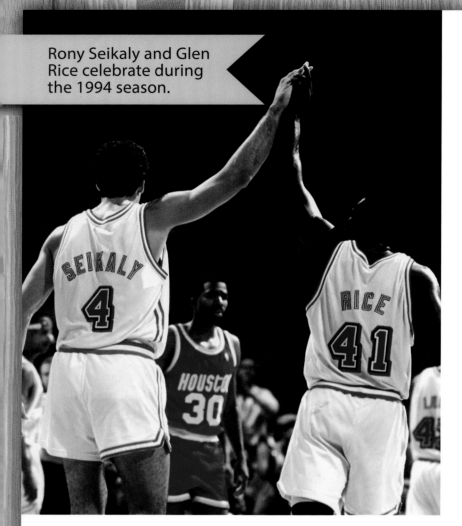

Rony Seikaly and Glen Rice celebrate during the 1994 season.

dribbled the ball up, guarded by Sparrow. With two seconds left, he shot a fadeaway jumpshot. The ball spun toward the rim, and then bounced off, giving the HEAT the 89-88 victory. The HEAT players and coaches stormed the court and celebrated.

"I forgot what it was like coming into a winning locker room," said Rony Seikaly, who had experienced great success during his college years at Syracuse.

Coach Ron Rothstein summed up the feeling in Miami: "It's a milestone day for our franchise and the city of

run the clock down, but committed a shot-clock violation. They turned the ball over to the Clippers with 12 seconds left, giving L.A. a chance to take the lead.

Clippers guard Norm Nixon

Miami. It hasn't been easy, but we've got a great group."

In their first season, the HEAT finished with a record of 15 wins and 67 losses.

Because of their struggles during the previous season, the HEAT received the fourth pick in the 1989 NBA Draft. With the pick, they chose Glen Rice, a superstar from the University of Michigan with one of the best shooting strokes ever. In Rice, the HEAT had a new top-notch talent. Rice averaged almost 20 points per game in six years with the team.

The HEAT showed improvement over their first few seasons, making the playoffs in 1991-92, and again in 1993-94. The young franchise was clearly on the rise.

He's on Fire!

In 1995, Glen Rice set Miami's franchise record for points in a game (56) against Orlando.

As the 1994-95 season ended, the HEAT were about to bring in a new coach. And with the new coach would come a new attitude. Even though they had played in the NBA for seven seasons, the HEAT were about to announce their presence to the rest of the league.

Glen Rice
to show
shootin

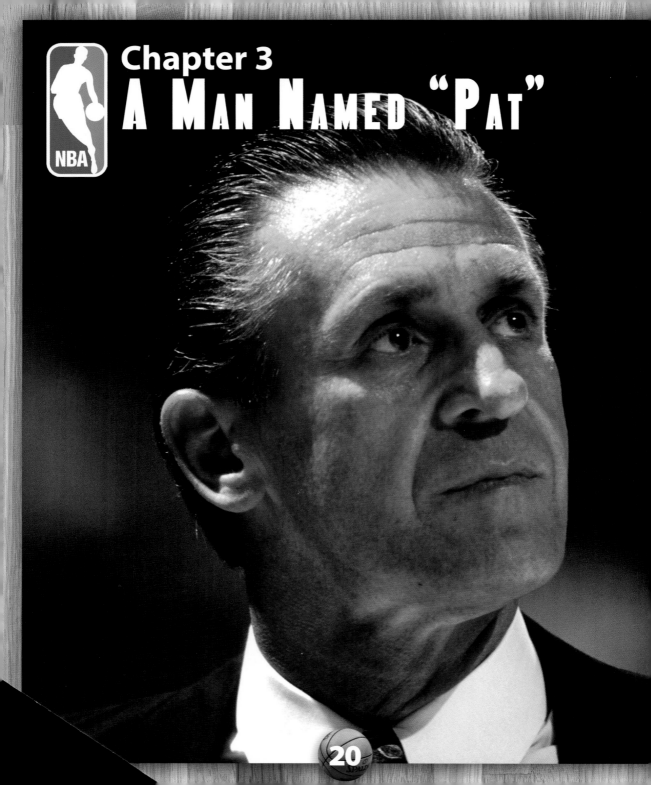

Chapter 3
A Man Named "Pat"

After the 1994-95 season, the HEAT's owners decided it was time for a change. For the HEAT to become a championship team, they felt they needed a coach who was already an NBA champion.

Pat Riley coached the Los Angeles Lakers for nine years, and the New York Knicks for four. His teams won four NBA Championships and eight conference titles during this time.

Riley was seen as a great coach for many reasons. In addition to the championships he won, he could coach teams with different styles. Riley's Lakers were fast and exciting. These high-scoring teams, led by Magic Johnson, were nicknamed "Showtime." But Riley's Knicks teams were different. Their best player was Patrick Ewing, and they were much

better on defense than offense. Riley found a way to win with both teams.

Pat Riley left the Knicks to coach the HEAT before the 1995-96 season. He was also named the team's general manager. Immediately, he started working to build a team he hoped could win a championship.

Pat Riley d
tenure as
the New

21

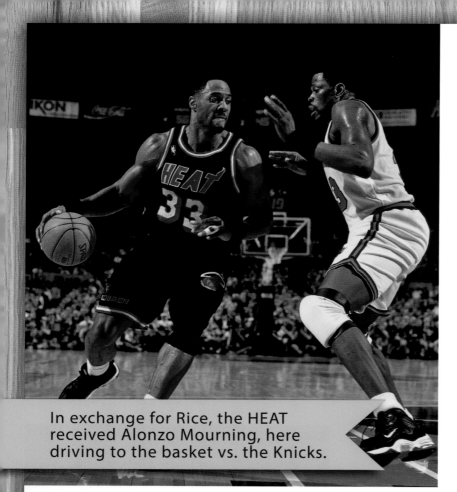

In exchange for Rice, the HEAT received Alonzo Mourning, here driving to the basket vs. the Knicks.

as an obvious one: who wouldn't trade the "concrete jungle" of New York for the palm trees and beaches of Miami?

Riley made an immediate splash when he arrived in Miami. He traded the HEAT's best player, Glen Rice, to the Charlotte Hornets. In exchange, the HEAT received All-Star center Alonzo Mourning. Mourning was similar to the biggest star on Riley's Knicks teams, Patrick Ewing. Both centers played their college ball at Georgetown. Both were terrific defensive players. Riley planned on building another tough, defensive

By bringing in Riley, the HEAT had created an immediate rivalry with New York. Fans of the Knicks believed Riley should have stayed there and finished the job of bringing a championship to New York.

HEAT fans viewed Riley's decision

team. He now had a key player in place.

In another big trade, Riley got Tim Hardaway, a talented point guard, from the Golden State Warriors.

The HEAT made a splash in Riley's second year with the team. They improved by 19 wins, and won the NBA's Atlantic Division. The HEAT even finished ahead of the Knicks. Both teams won their first round playoff series setting up a match-up between them in the Eastern Conference Semifinals.

The Knicks won three of the first four games. But an altercation during Game 5 led to the suspension of several key players. The momentum in the series shifted, and the HEAT were able to come back and win the hard-fought seven-game series.

If Riley's relocating from New York to Miami had begun the rivalry, beating the Knicks in the 1997 play-offs set the feud between the teams on fire. Every Knicks-HEAT game

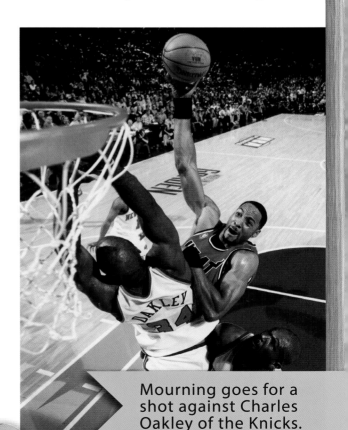

Mourning goes for a shot against Charles Oakley of the Knicks.

The HEAT's Tim Hardaway (left) watches teammate P.J. Brown and the Knicks' Charles Oakley (center) battle for a loose ball.

over the next few years would be a tough struggle.

The Knicks and HEAT faced each other again in the playoffs after each of the next three seasons. The Knicks won their series in 1998 and 1999. Each series was a physical clash, going the maximum number of games and often including pushing, shoving, and sometimes more.

Many fans consider their 2000 playoff series to be the best of them all. The HEAT won the Atlantic Division for the fourth straight year in 1999-2000. This time, the HEAT and Knicks didn't meet until the Eastern Conference Semifinals.

The teams split two close

games to open the series. The HEAT won Game 3 in overtime on a "circus shot" from rookie guard, Anthony Carter. Carter somehow managed to shoot the ball from behind the backboard and get it in the basket. The Knicks then won Game 4, 91-83. The teams split Games 5 and 6.

Again, the teams had "gone the distance," playing the maximum number of games in the series. Game 7 was a classic. In the final minutes, the HEAT took the lead on a three-pointer by Tim Hardaway. Then, Patrick Ewing gave the Knicks an 83-82 lead by dunking over his friend, Alonzo Mourning.

The HEAT's forward, Clarence Weatherspoon, had a chance to win the series at the very end. Weatherspoon was a no-nonsense forward typical of the players on the HEAT teams during this era. He looked like he might become a star

Carter makes an amazing shot from behind the backboard!

Familiar Foes
The HEAT and Knicks played against each other in 24 playoff games from 1997 to 2000.

as a young player with the 76ers, but instead found his niche as a solid NBA player. Never would he have a chance for glory, though, like the one he had at the end of Game 7.

With 12.4 seconds left, Dan Majerle inbounded the ball. Two passes later, Weatherspoon found himself with the ball and time running out. He extended his long arms and shot from about 12 feet away. The ball was on target. It looked like it might go in. But the ball hit the rim, bouncing off. The Knicks held on for another 2.1 seconds and won, 83-82.

"Of all the players on the court," said broadcaster Tom Hammond, "the last one you would guess to take a shot would be Clarence Weatherspoon."

Clarence Weatherspoon flushes in a slam dunk.

Even though no one knew it then, Weatherspoon's shot marked the end of this fierce period of rivalry between the HEAT and Knicks. Many of the players from these four series retired or left for other teams. While the HEAT would have many highlights in the first decade of the 21st century, the Knicks would go 12 years and counting without winning another playoff series.

A few years earlier, the HEAT were an expansion team. They had no history, and struggled to win games. Now, the Miami HEAT was one of the NBA's top franchises. Riley had brought a winning culture to the city. A trip to the playoffs was now expected at the end of every season.

And, even though they didn't know it yet, fans in Miami wouldn't

Coach Riley calls the shots from the sideline.

have to wait too much longer for their first trip to the NBA Finals.

A Unique View

Kurt Thomas saw the rivalry from both sides. He was on the HEAT bench during the 1997 playoffs, and was a key player for the Knicks in 1999 and 2000.

Chapter 4
A Championship Formula

After losing 57 games during the 2002-03 season, the HEAT received the fifth pick in the 2003 NBA Draft and selected Dwyane Wade.

A few months earlier, Wade had led his college team, the Marquette Golden Eagles, to the Final Four. This achievement showed HEAT executives that he was capable of leading his team to postseason success.

Wade grew up on the South Side of Chicago and rooted for Michael Jordan and the Bulls as a kid. Wade patterned his game after Jordan's, too. Like MJ, Wade didn't become a star until his junior year of high school. He had grown four inches the summer before and was now big enough to play shooting guard, the same position Jordan played.

Dwyane Wade was instrumental in bringing the Golden Eagles to the Final Four.

Drafting Wade was the first piece of a puzzle that Pat Riley hoped would lead the team to the NBA Finals.

A year later, Riley acquired a veteran star to play with the young

Midwest Kid
Dwyane Wade's college, Marquette University, is located in Milwaukee, Wisconsin.

and talented Wade.

There was no bigger star than Los Angeles Lakers center, Shaquille O'Neal. O'Neal was 7'1", with a personality just as big.

Since joining the league 12 years earlier, O'Neal had been the NBA's dominant force. He had played in 11 All-Star games and led the Lakers to three NBA Championships.

Could this combination of one young, budding star and one experienced, older one be the key to finally getting the HEAT to the NBA Finals? Fans in Miami expected a championship.

A season later, the HEAT found themselves in the 2006 NBA Finals. The series would begin with two games in Dallas against the Mavericks. The Mavericks were a deep and talented team and before they knew it,

Shaquille O'Neal holds up his new number 32 jersey flanked by coach Stan Van Gundy and Pat Riley.

the HEAT found themselves down 2-0. The HEAT left Dallas hoping they could use their home court to their advantage.

Game 3 in Miami didn't start much better for the HEAT. Wade had a brilliant performance, but the HEAT found themselves down by 13 with about six minutes left. No team had ever won the Finals after falling behind 3-0.

Dwyane Wade scored 12 points in the game's final minutes. Gary Payton, an NBA legend in a reserve role with the HEAT, hit the final basket. The HEAT earned a 98-96 win. Then the HEAT won Game 4 in a blowout, 98-74.

Gary Payton drives to the basket against the Dallas Mavericks.

Game 5 was a classic. Dwyane Wade scored 43 points and the HEAT won in overtime, 101-100. The HEAT were one win from their first NBA Championship.

Dwyane Wade shoots over Devin Harris in Game 5 of the 2006 NBA Finals.

to score. One defensive stop, and the HEAT would finally be champions.

Mavs guard Jason Terry dribbled the ball up the court. He was guarded closely by Gary Payton. Terry advanced over half court. He went to his right. Payton stayed right with him. Dirk Nowitzki set a pick to give Terry room to take a shot. Terry dribbled past. He elevated, and put up a jumper from behind the three-point line.

When the series moved back to Dallas, Game 6 was another close one. With only eight seconds left, the HEAT held a 95-92 lead. The Mavericks had one final chance

It went up... Fans in the crowd, nearly all of them wearing white, held their collective breath.

It was on target... Would the HEAT come so close to glory once more, only to find the bitter taste of defeat?

It hit the rim and bounced up… Maybe this would be the moment fans had waited nearly 20 years for…

…And bounced away into the hands of Wade. Wade dribbled twice as time ran out.

The HEAT were NBA champions! Finally, they were at the top of the league. Veterans like Mourning, Payton, and Shaq celebrated with the younger players like Wade and Haslem. Riley had done it again, and victory was sweet. The city of Miami doesn't ever need an excuse to party. On that special night, the

Riley and his team celebrate the championship.

city of Miami celebrated the HEAT's championship like they never had before!

Trifecta Part II
Pat Riley is the only coach to take three different teams to the NBA Finals: the Lakers, Knicks, and HEAT.

Chapter 5

A FRANCHISE ON FIRE

After coming so close to their second championship in 2010-11, the 2011-12 Miami HEAT were determined to win it all.

The HEAT's "Big Three" had all been picked early in the 2003 NBA Draft. They had played in the Beijing Olympics together and won a gold medal. Now LeBron James, Dwyane Wade, and Chris Bosh wanted to win a championship. They all had something to prove.

James came into the season as one of the most accomplished NBA players never to win a title. Wade had received plenty of individual awards, but craved another title. And Bosh had been known for most of

Big Season
LeBron James won the regular season and NBA Finals MVP awards in 2011-12.

his career as a good player on bad teams. This was the season to prove all of the doubters wrong.

HEAT coach Erik Spoelstra had as much to prove as any of his players. Spoelstra isn't your typical NBA head coach. Spoelstra didn't come into the league as a coach. He joined

Wade, Bosh, and James sit on the bench together in a game during the 2008 Olympics in Beijing.

35

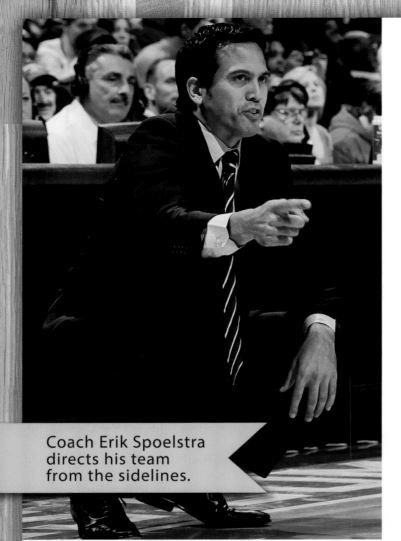

Coach Erik Spoelstra directs his team from the sidelines.

At the time he was named to the position, Spoelstra was the youngest head coach in the NBA. Spoelstra is also the first Asian-American head coach in NBA history. Coach Spoelstra's mother is from the Philippines, an island country in Southeast Asia.

Mario Chalmers' defense and floor leadership were key to the HEAT's success in the 2011-12 season. His talent for playing under pressure helped his Kansas Jayhawks team win a national championship during his junior year in college.

the HEAT in 1995 as their video coordinator. He worked his way up through the organization, and when Pat Riley stepped down in 2008, he named Spoelstra as his replacement.

Before the season, the HEAT wanted to add an experienced veteran who could shoot and play tough defense. They got exactly what they wanted in Shane Battier. Like Chalmers, Battier was an NCAA champion while at Duke University. In 11 NBA seasons, Battier became known as a true professional.

Udonis Haslem was the only player, besides Dwyane Wade, still left from the HEAT's 2006 NBA Championship team. He does the "little things" on the court that many players are not prone to do. He fights for rebounds, sets picks and plays tough defense.

Mike Miller, one of the most accurate three-point shooters in league history, came off the HEAT

After only connecting on 62 all season, Shane Battier hit 15 three-pointers during the 2012 NBA Finals.

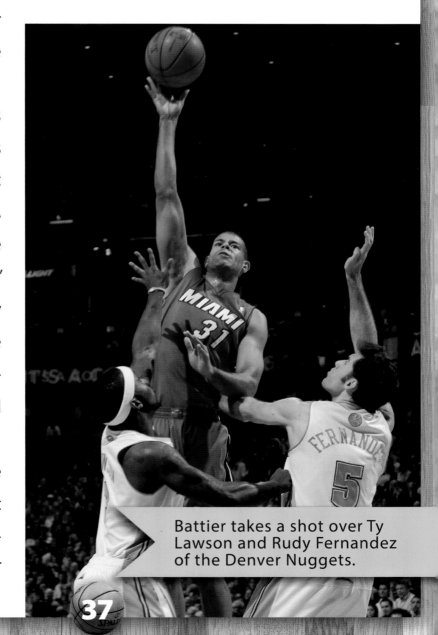

Battier takes a shot over Ty Lawson and Rudy Fernandez of the Denver Nuggets.

bench when they needed a big shot in 2011-12.

For most of the 2011-12 season, the HEAT's starting center was Joel Anthony. Anthony is one of six players in the NBA who was born in Canada. Anthony is known for his shot-blocking and rebounding ability with the HEAT. But on the Canadian National Team, Anthony is one of the top scorers.

The HEAT had a terrific regular season, winning 46 games, the second best win total in the Eastern Conference.

LeBron James averaged 27

Anthony attempts to block a shot from Spencer Hawes against the Philadelphia 76ers.

points, 7.9 rebounds, 6.2 assists, and 1.9 steals per game. He won the league's MVP award for the third time in his career.

LeBron James in action against the Knicks.

The first round of the 2012 NBA Playoffs matched the HEAT against their old foes, the Knicks. Unlike their series in the past, this Knicks team was no match for the HEAT who won the series easily, four games to one. All four of Miami's wins were by double digits, including a 33-point thrashing in Game 1. Miami's margin of victory in their four wins was an impressive 18 points. The Knicks' lone victory in Game 4 was by a narrow 2-point margin.

Next up were the Indiana Pacers, a team with a balanced attack, and a deeper rotation than the HEAT. The HEAT would have to compete in this series without one of their stars. Chris Bosh went down with an injury in Game 1 and wouldn't return for a couple of weeks.

Playing Against His Idol
Chris Bosh's favorite player growing up was Kevin Garnett.

The HEAT lost two of the first three games and looked to be on the verge of a disastrous finish to their season. But, just as things looked darkest, the HEAT rallied.

After having one of the worst

Dwyane Wade creates room for a shot over George Hill in the 2012 NBA Playoffs.

playoff games of his life in Game 3, Dwyane Wade scored 30 in Game 4 and the HEAT evened the series. From there, the HEAT put on a dominant performance at home in Game 5, winning 115-83. The HEAT wrapped up the series in Indiana two nights later.

Now, they headed to the Eastern Conference Finals against the Boston Celtics. The HEAT were able to take a commanding two-game lead on the experienced Celtics. They won Game 1 easily, and Game 2 in overtime.

But, just as it looked like the HEAT would cruise to victory, they lost three straight games to the savvy Celtics.

In Game 6, LeBron James had one of the best playoff performances of

Chalmers in action against the Celtics.

all time, finishing with 45 points and 15 rebounds. He carried his team when they needed it most and led the HEAT back to Miami.

Game 7 was close for three quarters, but the HEAT pulled away in the fourth. Chris Bosh, back since Game 5, finally made a significant impact on the series, scoring 19 points and helping to send the HEAT back to the NBA Finals.

YO (AL)MARIO?!
Mario Chalmers real first name is "Almario."

The Thunder's Kevin Durant dunks in Game 1 of the NBA Finals

Durant is considered by many to be the league's best pure scorer. And Russell Westbrook may be the NBA's best all-around athlete.

The HEAT were out-played in Game 1 and fell behind in the series imme-diately. Miami's defense was weak and Durant and Westbrook combined for 41 points—more than the entire HEAT team—in the second half.

The HEAT came out on fire in Game 2, building an 18-2 lead to start the game. But over the next three quarters, the Thunder battled back. Kevin Durant had a chance to tie the game in the final seconds but his shot bounced off the rim and the

Standing between the HEAT and the NBA title were the Oklahoma City Thunder. The Thunder boasted two of the league's brightest stars and a strong supporting cast as well. Kevin

Back to Work

Only weeks after the Finals ended, LeBron James and three members of the Thunder became teammates on the 2012 U.S. Olympic team.

HEAT won, 100-96.

The HEAT didn't shoot well in Game 3 in Miami, and fell behind by 10 in the third quarter. But, Miami played strong defense to keep themselves in the game. James and Wade combined for 54 points and the HEAT won it, 91-85.

Game 4 was one of the most dramatic NBA Finals contests ever. The game featured an all-time performance (the Thunder's Russell Westbrook scored 43 points), an unlikely hero (Mario Chalmers finished with 25, tying his career postseason best), and a heart-stopping finish.

After nearly putting up a triple-double, LeBron James got leg cramps late in the fourth quarter and could barely walk. LeBron came out

Wade makes his move against the Thunder in Game 5.

James's three-point shot won Game 4 for the HEAT.

of the game for a short rest, but limped right back in.

With the score tied and three minutes left, James dribbled at the top of the key. He could barely walk, much less drive to the hoop, so he put up a three-pointer. His shot swished, landing at the bottom of the net and giving the HEAT a 98-95 lead that they would never give up. The series was now 3-1 in their favor.

"That three was just sheer will and competitiveness, to contribute in some way," coach Spoelstra said.

Before a crazed crowd, everyone wearing white, the HEAT took the floor for Game 5. LeBron declared that he was taking a "Game 7 mentality" into the contest, knowing that sending the series back to Oklahoma City was a risk the HEAT couldn't afford.

While the first four games of the series had been tight, closely contested games, there was no stopping the HEAT in Game 5. They

built a 10-point halftime lead and never let up, knowing that backing off even a little could spell disaster. The HEAT won the 2012 NBA Championship with a final score of 121-106.

LeBron celebrates winning his first NBA Championship.

As players and coaches shared hugs on the sidelines, LeBron James watched the closing seconds and jumped up and down on the sidelines in utter joy.

The rest of the night was a party that Miami had been waiting for ever since the controversy of "The Decision." Commissioner David Stern handed the trophy to HEAT owner Micky Arison. Pat Riley gleefully addressed the crowd. And Stern named LeBron James the MVP of the NBA Finals.

"It was a journey," James said. "Everything that went along with me being a high school prodigy when I was 16 years old and on the cover of Sports Illustrated, to being drafted and having to be the face of a franchise, and everything that came with it. I had to deal with it, and I had to learn through it. No one had gone through that journey, and I had to learn on my own. I can finally say that I'm a champion."

In only a few short months, the HEAT would

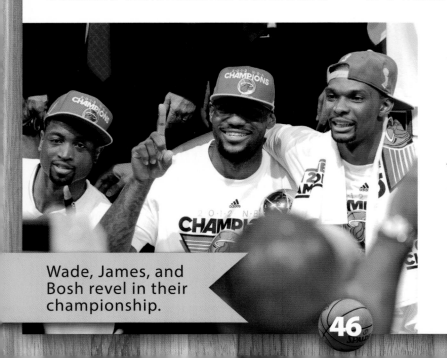

Wade, James, and Bosh revel in their championship.

The team celebrates around the Larry O'Brien Championship Trophy.

be back on the court to start all over. Was the 2011-12 NBA title the start of a Miami HEAT dynasty? Only time would tell.

But for now, the city of Miami can celebrate their place at the top of the basketball world. The Miami HEAT are, undeniably, a franchise on fire!

New Blood

During the 2012 NBA Draft, the HEAT picked up Justin Hamilton, a seven-footer out of Louisiana State University.